SpringerBriefs in Computer Science

T0185146

Series Editors

Stan Zdonik
Peng Ning
Shashi Shekhar
Jonathan Katz
Xindong Wu
Lakhmi C. Jain
David Padua
Xuemin Shen
Borko Furht
V. S. Subrahmanian
Martial Hebert
Katsushi Ikeuchi
Bruno Siciliano

For further volumes:
http://www.springer.com/series/10028

Bernard P. Zeigler

Guide to Modeling and Simulation of Systems of Systems

User's Reference

 Springer

Bernard P. Zeigler
Chief Scientist
RTSync Corp
Rockville, MD
USA

ISSN 2191-5768   ISSN 2191-5776   (electronic)
ISBN 978-1-4471-4569-1   ISBN 978-1-4471-4570-7   (eBook)
DOI 10.1007/978-1-4471-4570-7
Springer London Heidelberg New York Dordrecht

Library of Congress Control Number: 2012946625

Printed on acid-free paper

Springer is part of Springer Science+Business Media (www.springer.com)

To Doohwan Kim, Chungman Seo, Robert Coop, and Phillip Hammonds whose dedication, hard work, and expertise brought the DEVS concept to its realization in the MS4 Modeling Environment[TM]

Preface

"Guide to Modeling and Simulation of Systems of Systems" explicates integrated development environments to support virtual building and testing of Systems of Systems. As focal point of such environments, the MS4 Modeling Environment™ (ms4systems.com), is covered in some depth. This user's reference provides a quick reference and exposition of the various concepts and functional features covered in the book.

The MS4 Modeling Environment™ opens with the launch page shown below with a default workflow for using the tools and objects required for System of Systems modeling and simulation.

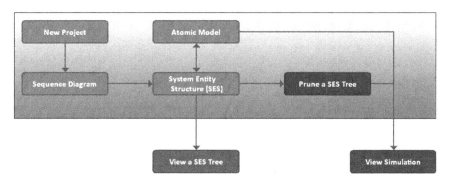

This reference collects together and organizes the various concepts and features discussed in "Guide to Modeling and Simulation of Systems of Systems." In alignment with the launch page the reference collects features grouped under headings, Atomic Models, System Entity Structure, Pruning SES, and Miscellaneous. If you know the category of a feature you are looking up you can go to the corresponding grouping; if not, you can look up the feature alphabetically in the Index.

Each feature is explicated under the headings: Why use it, When to use it, How to use it, and Other Comments. Links to related features are also included.

Contents

Chapter 1
Atomic Models List

Abstract This chapter lists statements for creating and manipulating atomic models in the MS4 Modeling Environment™. The statements relate to using the constrained natural language for defining Finite Deterministic DEVS models and enhancing these models using tagged code blocks. These blocks add java code to the appropriate slots in the java classes that are autogenerated from the natural language specifications.

1.1 Topic: The "Accepts Input" Statement for FDDEVS

Why use it:

This statement adds an input port to the model which enables proper handling of external events set up by "whenIn" statements. Providing the type of the value to appear on a port enables the system to check at compile time whether values that are assigned to the port are of the specified type.

When to use it:

Write this statement after you have created a new state in a *.dnl file and you wish to use an input port in an external transition, i.e., when you wish to use the. input port in a "whenIn" statement.

How to use it:

Write the statement in a *.dnl file:

The statement takes two forms:

1. Form 1

```
accepts input on <input port> with type <port type>!
```

where <input port> is the name of the port and <port type> is the Java type assigned to it.

Note the input port created in the atomic model Java class file, and used in the simulation prefixes "in" to the <input port>

For example,

```
accepts input on Job with type WorkToDo!
```

B. P. Zeigler, *Guide to Modeling and Simulation of Systems of Systems*,
SpringerBriefs in Computer Science, DOI: 10.1007/978-1-4471-4570-7_1,

will result in a declaration of an input port "inJob" with type WorkToDo in the Java file.

2. Form 2

```
accepts input on <input port>!
```

where <input port> is the name of the port and the port type defaults to type Serializable.class.

Note the input port created in the atomic model Java class file and used in the simulation prefixes "in" to the <input port>

For example,

```
accepts input on Job!
```

will result in a declaration of an input port "inJob" with type Serializable.class in the Java file.

Other Comments:

- You can use simple data types such as String, Integer, and Double as well as Java classes as port types.
- To see how to define a Java class to provide as type for a port, go to the entry "Java Class Definition."
- The Serializable.class that is assigned as port type by default is very accepting since many common types are sub-classed to it.

1.2 Topic: The "After" Statement in FDDEVS

Why use it:

This statement allows you to tell the model to output on a specific output port after its time has elapsed in the current state.

When to use it:

Write this statement after you have created a new state.

How to use it:

The statement has the form:

```
after <someState> output <Port>!
```

Which tells the model that after its time has expired in <someState> it should place an output on port out<Port>.
Note that the time it spends in <someState> should be set by a "hold in" statement.

Other Comments:

- A passive state (for which resting time is infinity) does not have an "after" assignment.
- There should be only one "after" statement for every non-passive state.

1.3 Topic: External Event Tagged Code Block

Why use it:

The atomic models generated by FDDEVS by default only send and receive strings of portNames. Declaring port types and using tagged code blocks allows you to send and receive structured data types that are more attuned to your model's needs.

When to use it:

Add an external event tagged block to the *.dnl file to receive data after you have defined a Java class and output event tagged block to send structured data.

How to use it:

In the tagged block for the phase and input port you can get the value arriving through an external event on that port. To do this note that the messages arriving on an input port are available by processing a variable called messageList, specifically for that port. Then to get the first value on that port, we get the first message and its data. Corresponding to the statements:

```
accepts input on <input port> with type <type>!
when in <current state> and receive <input port> go to <next
state>!
```

write the tagged code block

```
external event for <current state> with <input port>
<%
(type)value = messageList.get(0).getData();
%>!
```

to get the first element on the list of values on <input port>.

For example, having the statements:

```
accepts input on Job with type WorkToDo!
when in waitForJob and receive Job go to sendJob!
```

write the tagged block

```
external event for waitForJob with Job
<%
WorkToDo job = messageList.get(0).getData();
%>!
```

where WorkToDo is a class already defined.

Other Comments:

- To see how define an external transition go to the entry "whenIn."
- To see how to define a Java class go to the entry "Java Class Definition."
- To see how to declare a port type for input go to the entry "Accepts input" statement.

1.4 Topic: The Finite Deterministic DEVS Model

Why use it:

Finite Deterministic DEVS (FDDEVS) models provide easier user-friendly means to define atomic models than writing directly in code. They are automatically transformed into coded form.

When to use it:

Define an FDDEVS model when you need to create an atomic model that can run on its own and later be extended to greater behavioral complexity.

How to use it:

- Create a *.dnl file and write statements into it using the editor.
- Individual statements are discussed on separate pages.
- When you save the file, it will automatically generate an Atomic Model *.java file with the same name as the *.dnl file.
- The automatically generated java files are found in the Models.java folder with the current project.

Other Comments:

Compare the statements with the corresponding features in the corresponding java files to gain a thorough understanding of how they fit together.

1.5 Topic: The "From … go to" Statement in FDDEVS

Why use it:

This statement allows you to tell the model to transition to a specific state after its time has elapsed in the current state.

When to use it:

Write this statement after you have created a new state in a *.dnl file.

How to use it:

The statement has the form:

```
from <some state> go to <some other state>!
```

For example,

```
from Running go to idle!
```

which tells the model that after its time has expired in Running it should transition to the idle state. Note that the time it spends in Running should be set by a "hold in" statement.

Other Comments:

- A passive state (for which resting time is infinity) does not have a "from" assignment.
- There should be only one "from" statement for every non-passive state. In contrast, there can be any number of "when in" statements for <some state> that contain "go to."
- For elaborating an internal transition go to "Internal event tagged code block."

1.6 Topic: The "Generates Output" Statement for FDDEVS

Why use it:

This statement adds an output port to the model which enables proper handling of output events set up by "after" statements. Providing the type of the value to appear on a port enables the system to check at compile time whether values that are assigned to the port are of the specified type.

When to use it:

Write this statement after you have created a new state in a *.dnl file and you wish to use an output port in an output function, i.e., when you wish to use the. output port in an "after" statement.

How to use it:

Write the statement in a *.dnl file:

The statement takes two forms:

1. Form 1

```
generates output on <output port> with type <port type>!
```

where <output port> is the name of the port and <port type> is the Java type assigned to it.

Note the output port created in the atomic model Java class file and used in the simulation prefixes "out" to the <output port>

For example,

```
generates output on Job with type WorkToDo!
```

will result in a declaration of an output port "outJob" with type WorkToDo in the Java file.

2. Form 2

```
generates output on <output port>!
```

where <output port> is the name of the port and the port type defaults to type Serializable.class.

Note the output port created in the atomic model Java class file and used in the simulation prefixes "out" to the `<output port>`

For example,

```
generates output on Job!
```

will result in a declaration of an output port "outJob" with type Serializable.class in the Java file.

Other Comments:

- You can use simple data types such as String, Integer, and Double as well as Java classes as port types.
- To see how to define a Java class to provide as type for a port, go to the entry "Java Class Definition."
- The Serializable.class that is assigned as port type by default is very accepting since many common types are sub-classed to it.

1.7 Topic: The "Hold in" Statement in FDDEVS

Why use it:

This statement allows you to say how long the model stays in a specific state.

When to use it:

Write this statement after you have created a new state in a model's *.dnl file.

How to use it:

This statement has two forms:

1. Form 1

```
to start passivate in <some state>!
```

For example,

```
passivate in idle!
```

which tells the model to stay in the idle state forever or until it receives an input.

2. Form 2:

```
hold in <some state> for <some time>!
```

For example,

```
hold in Running for time 100!
```

which tells the model to stay in the Running state for 100 time units or until it receives an input.

Other Comments:

- There should be only one "hold in" statement for every state.
- A state is said to be passive if Form 1 is used for it. This is the same as giving it a resting time of infinity.

1.8 Topic: Internal Event Tagged Code Block

Why use it:

This statement allows you to fill in the internal transition to a specific state after its time has elapsed in the current state.

When to use it:

Add a tagged code block for internal event in a *.dnl file when you wish to elaborate on the detailed processing in an internal transition.

How to use it:

In the internal event tagged block for the phase you can write java code to operate on the state of the model. Corresponding to the statements:

```
from <current state> go to <next state>!
```

write the tagged code block

```
internal event for <current state>
<%
//Java code to operate on the model's state
%>!
```

For example, having the statement:

```
from generate go to generate!
```

write the tagged block

```
internal event for generate
<%
//Java code to prepare for next generated output
%>!
```

Other Comments:

• To see how to define an internal transition go to the entry "From...GoTo."

1.9 Topic: Output Event Tagged Code Block

Why use it:

The atomic models generated by FDDEVS by default only send and receive strings of portNames. Declaring port types and using tagged code blocks allows you to send and receive structured data types that are more attuned to your model's needs.

When to use it:

Add an output event tagged block to the *.dnl file to send data after you have defined a Java class and a typed port to support this output.

How to use it:

In the tagged block for the phase you can send the value by adding it to the output messageBag. Corresponding to the statements:

```
generates output on <output port> with type <type>!
after <current state> output <output port>!
```

write the tagged code block

```
output event for <current state>
<%
output.add (out<output port> value);
%>!
```

where value is an instance of type <type>.

For example, having the statements:

```
generates output on Job with type WorkToDo!
after sendJob output Job!
```

write the tagged block

```
output event for sendJob
<%
output.add(outJob,value);
%>!
```

where value is an instance of WorkToDo.

Other Comments:

- To see how to define an output from a state go to the entry "After."!
- To see how to define a Java class go to the entry "Java Class Definition."
- To see how to declare a port type for output go to the entry "Generates output" statement.

1.10 Topic: The "To Start" Statement in FDDEVS

Why use it:

Every model has to start in a given state - this statement allows you to say what that state is.

When to use it:

Write this statement when you begin a new atomic model in its *.dnl file.

How to use it:

This statement has two forms:

1. Form 1

```
to start passivate in <some state>!
```

For example,

```
to start passivate in idle!
```

which tells the model to start in idle and stay there forever or until it receives an input.

2. Form 2:

```
to start hold in <some state> for <some time>!
```

For example,

```
to start hold in idle for time 100!
```

which tells the model to start in idle and stay there for 100 time units or until it receives an input.

Other Comments:

- There should be one, and only one, "to start" statement in a model's *.dnl file.
- A state is said to be passive if it if Form 1 is used for it. This is the same as giving it a resting time of infinity

1.11 Topic: Declaring (State) Instance Variables in FDDEVS Elaboration

Why use it:

Atomic models that are generated from FDDEVS natural language do not have memory storage beyond the finite states they define. To provide the full capability of DEVS, you want to give memory storage to atomic models. Declare an instance variable if you need to keep track of structured data in the state of a model.

When to use it:

Declare an instance variable after you have developed an atomic model and wish to work with complex data as part of the model's state.

How to use it:

In a *.dnl file write

```
use <InstVar> with type <type> and default "<defaultValue>"!
```

The *.java that is automatically generated will declare the <InstVar> as an instance variable with the given <type> and <defaultValue>. For example, writing

```
use wtd with type WorkToDo and default "new WorkToDo()"!
```

in the *.dnl file will result in the declaration:

```
protected WorkToDo wtd = new WorkToDo();
```

and
the assignment within the initialize() method:

```
wtd = new WorkToDo();
```

in the *.java file

Other Comments:

To see how to declare a Java class, go to the entry "Java Class Definition."

1.12 Topic: The "When in" Statement in FDDEVS

Why use it:

This statement allows you to say what the model does when it receives a specific input.

When to use it:

Write this statement when you want to create an input port and a model response to inputs on that port.

How to use it:

The statement has two forms:

1. Form 1: (by far the most commonly used one)

```
when in <some state> and receive <input> go to <some other
state>!
```

as in IntroFDDEVS1.dnl:

```
when in idle and receive Start go to Running!
```

This tells the model

- that there is an input port called inStart and that
- when in state idle and an input is received on the toStart port it should immediately transition to state Running.

2. Form 2:

```
when in <some state> and receive <input> go to <some other
state> eventually!
```

as in

```
when in Running and receive Stop go to Finishing eventually!
```

This tells the model the same information as does Form 1, except that the additional "eventually" has the effect of delayings its transition to occur at the same time it was scheduled for by the "hold in" assignment associated with Finishing. (This also delays any output to occur later as well.)

Other Comments:

- There can be any number of "when in" statements.
- However, there should be only one <some other state> specified for a given pair of <some state> and <input> values.
- It is allowed that <some other state> is the same as <some state>, but such a transition back to itself under some input is rarely used.

Chapter 2
System Entity Structure List

Abstract This chapter lists statements for creating and manipulating System Entity Structures in the MS4 Modeling Environment™. The statements relate to using the constrained natural language for defining such structures including their component entities, aspects, couplings, specializations, and variables.

2.1 Topic: The "All sends to all" Statement in SES

Why use it:

This statement tells how to couple individuals of two groups of components derived from restructuring.

When to use it:

Write this statement when you want to couple output ports of components of a group in the same way to receivers of a second (possibly the same) group.

This statement is the same as writing the "One sends to all" statement for each component in the group.

How to use it:

Write the statement into a *.ses file.

The statement has two forms:

1. Form 1:

```
From the <perspective> perspective, all <component1> sends <Message>
to all <component2>!
```

where <component1> and <component2> should already have been specified as component derived by restructuting of a multiaspect in the <perspective> (see the "Restructure SES" entry.)

<Message> can be any alphabetic string; a matching pair of output and input ports are auto-generated if they do not already exist.

For example,

```
From the game perspective, all Boy sends Hello to all Boy!
From the game perspective, all Girl sends Hello to all Girl!
From the game perspective, all Girl sends NiceToMeetYou to all
Boy!
```

which says that

- all boys greet each other with Hello
- all girls greet each other with Hello
- every girl say NiceToMeetYou to every boy

2. Form 2:

```
From   the <perspective> perspective,   all <component1> sends
<outPort> to all <component2> as <inPort>!
```

Here <outPort> and <inPort> are output and input ports of <component1> and <component2> respectively.

Other Comments:

This statement is the same as writing the "One sends to all" statement for each component in the group.

2.2 Topic: The "All sends to One" Statement in SES

Why use it:

This is the reverse of the statement "One sends to all"—it relates every component of a same type to a receiver.

When to use it:

Write this statement when you want to couple output ports of components of a group in the same way to a receiver.

How to use it:

The statement has two forms:

1. Form 1:

```
From   the <perspective>   perspective,   all   <component>   sends
<Message> to <component or coupled model>!
```

where <component> should already have been specified as a component derived by restructuring of a multiaspect in the <perspective> (see the "Restructure SES" entry.)

<Message> can be any alphabetic string -a matching pair of output and input ports are auto-generated if they do not already exist.

For example,

```
From the game perspective, all Player sends Ready to Simon!
```

which says that each Player's output port outReady is coupled to Simons's input port inReady.

2. Form 2:

```
From the <perspective> perspective, all <component1> sends
<outPort> to <component or coupled model> as <inPort>!

Here <outPort> and <inPort> are output and input ports of
<component1> and <component2> respectively.
```

Other Comments:

2.3 Topic: The "Can be" (Specialization) Statement in SES

Why use it:

Use this statement to introduce an element of choice into the components of a coupled model.

This use allows you to specify alternative choices for a component that can be made in pruning.

You can then think of a component as a place holder into which one of the alternatives can be "plugged."

When to use it:

Use this kind of statement when you want to specify alternative forms or variants of a component.

How to use it:

Enter the "can be" statement in a *.ses file:

The statement has two forms:

1. Form 1:

```
<component> can be <alternative1>,<alternative2>, <alternative>,…
in <specialization>!
```

where <component> should already have been specified as an entity in an aspect or specialization.

Note that <specialization> should be a name suggestive of a family of choices, e.g., color, gender, etc.

For example,

```
GeneratorOfJobs can be Fast or Slow in speed!
```

which says that the GeneratorOfJobs has two alternative plug-in behaviors: Fast and Slow.

2. Form 2:

```
<component> is like <another component> in <specialization>!
```

For example,

```
ProcessorOfJobs is like GeneratorOfJobs in speed!
```

which says that `ProcessorOfJobs` has the same specialization, speed, as `GeneratorOfJobs`.

Other Comments:

- Note that Form 2 refers back to Form 1 to give the same choices for a different component.
- You can also explicitly write the desired equivalent specialization.
- For example, you can write:

```
ProcessorOfJobs can be Fast or Slow in speed!
```

In either case, this allows independent selection of behavior from the two entities.
- See the "Select Specialization" topic for details.

2.4 Topic: Coupling Specification for Multi-aspect Models

Why use it:

Just as restructuring a multi-aspect using a specialization with multiplicity setting allows you to determine the number components when pruning, so Coupling Specification allows you to specify couplings for the components also at the time of pruning.

When to use it:

Apply this construct to specify a coupling recipe declaratively rather than manually.

How to use it:

1. Step 1:

In a *.ses file add one or more coupling specifications as components to a coupled model containing a multi-aspect.

```
From the <perspective> perspective, <coupled model> is made of
<components>, <identifier1> CouplingSpecification,…, and <identifi-
erN> CouplingSpecification!
```

where <components> has a multi-aspect decomposition using a specialization that will be expanded.

For example:

```
From the cell perspective, cellspace is made of cells, cellEW-
CouplingSpecification, and cellNSCouplingSpecification!
```

```
From the multiCell perspective, cells is made of more than one
cell!

cell can be x or y in location!
```

2. Step 2:

In a *.pes file, after "restructuring" and "set multiplicity" statements, write statements of the form:

```
write <specification type> specification for <component> and
<specialization> based on <identifier>!
for <identifier> leftnode sends <message> to rightnode!
...
```

where <component> is the multi-entity of <components>, <specialization> is the specialization to be expanded, <identifier> is the identifier used to identify this coupling specification in the SES, <message> is a port of your choice (there may be any number of these messages), and <specification type> is a designation for an available type of coupling specification, such as "cycle", cellular" or "tree".

For example:

after the statements:

```
restructure multi-aspects using location!
set multiplicity of location as [3,3] for cell!
```

you wrte:

```
write cellular specification for cell and location based on
cellEW!
for cellEW leftnode sends East to rightnode!
for cellEW rightnode sends West to leftnode!
```

This sets up a coupling pattern in which cells communicate with their immediate neighbors to the east and west using ports labeled outEast, inEast, outWest, and inWest.

There is also a specification identified by cellNS, that sets up a similar north–south pattern.

Other Comments:

You can also spell out your own detailed couplings. To do this you use the more generic statement:

```
write coupling specification for <component> and <specialization>
based on <identifier>!
```

and spell out the actual pairs of nodes to be coupled using

```
add   coupling <identifier> pair   from <node1> to <node2> in
:specialization>!
```

For example, if in the *.ses file you have:

```
From the net perspective, mynet is made of MYOWNCouplingSpeci-
fication and nodeElements!
```

```
From the mult perspective, nodeElements is made of more than
one nodeElement!
nodeElement can be u1, u2, u3, or u4 in index!
```

then in the *.pes file you can write:

```
restructure multiaspects using index!
write coupling specification for nodeElement and index based on
MYOWN!
for MYOWN leftnode sends Hello to rightnode!
add coupling MYOWNpair from u1 to u2 in index!
add coupling MYOWNpair from u2 to u3 in index!
```

2.5 Topic: The "Each sends to each" Statement in SES

Why use it:

This statement tells how to couple individuals of two groups of components derived from restructuring.

When to use it:

Write this statement when you want to couple output ports of components of a group in a one–one manner to receivers of a second (possibly the same) group.

How to use it:

Write the statement into a *.ses file.

The statement has two forms:

1. Form 1:

```
From the <perspective> perspective,   each <component1> sends
<Message> to each <component2>!
```

where <component1> and <component2> should already have been specified as component derived by restructuting of a multiaspect in the <perspective>> (see the "Restructure SES" entry.)

<Message> can be any alphabetic string - a matching pair of ouput and input ports are auto-generated if it does not already exist.

```
From the game perspective, each Boy sends Invitation to each
Girl!
```

which says that boys send invitations to girls in a one–one manner.

The one–one correspondence is based on matching of the values of the specialization underlying the restructuring.

In this case, boys and girls might be matched up by having the same height, e.g., tall_Boy is coupled to tall_Girl, etc. if height were the underlying specialization.

2. Form 2:

```
From the <perspective> perspective, each <component1> sends <out-
Port> to each <component2> as <inPort>!
```

where <component1> and <component2> should already have been specified as components derived by restructuring of a multiaspect in the <perspective>.

Other Comments:

The matching algorithm looks for a receiver having the same prefix (before the underscore) as the sender; if the specializations are not the same, then only some, or perhaps none, of the senders will have a match.

2.6 Topic: The "Each sends to one" Statement in SES

Why use it:

This is the reverse of the statement "One sends to each" - it relates every component of a same type to a single receiver.

When to use it:

Write this statement when you want to couple output ports of components of a group to a receiver in a sender-specific manner.

How to use it:

Write the statement into a *.ses file.

The statement has two forms:

1. Form 1:

```
From   the <perspective> perspective,   each <component> sends
<Message> to <component or coupled model>!
```

where <component> should already have been specified as a component derived by restructuring of a multiaspect in the <perspective> (see the "Restructure SES" entry.).

<Message> can be any alphabetic string; a matching pair of output and input ports are auto-generated if they do not already exist.

For example,

```
From the game perspective, each Player sends Comply to Simon!
```

which says that each Player's output port outComply is coupled to Simons's input port <player> _inComply.

Note that the stamping, for example, Alice_inComply of each player's identity on Simon's input port allows Simon to identify the sources of inputs on the same port.

2. Form 2:

> From the <perspective> perspective, each <component> sends <outPort>
> to <component or coupled model> as <inPort>!

Here <outPort> and <inPort> are output and input ports of <component1> and <component> respectively.

Other Comments:

2.7 Topic: The "Made of" Statement in SES

Why use it:

This statement tells how a modeled component is made of, or composed from, more basic components. Alternatively, it tells how the entity representing a component is decomposed into smaller entities using the aspect relation..

When to use it:

Write this statement when you want to define a coupled model whose components are atomic or other coupled models.

How to use it:

Write this statement in a *.ses file.

The statement has the form:

> From the <perspective> perspective, the <coupled model> is made
> of <component1>, <component2>, <component3>, and <component4>!

Here there should be at least one component listed after "made of", each separated by a comma.

For example,

> From the play perspective, the SimonSaysGame is made of Simon,
> Alice, Bill, and Charlie!

which says that a coupled model named "SimonSaysGame" is to be generated from the SES and which has components named Simon, Alice, Bill, and Charlie.

The <perspective>, in this case "play", provides a name for this particular way of constructing the SimonSaysGame.

Other Comments:

- There should be only one "made of" statement with a particular <perspective> for a particular entity (two such statements would amount to giving two different sets of components for the same composition).
- However, there can be many "made of" statements with different perspectives which represent different ways of constructing coupled models with the given name.

2.8 Topic: The "Sends to all" Statement in SES

Why use it:

A series of these statements tells how the output ports of a component or the input ports of a coupled model are coupled to input ports of components that are all of the same type.

When to use it:

Write this kind of statement when you want to specify how an output port of a component or input port of a coupled model is coupled to the input port of components that are all of the same type.

How to use it:

Write the statement into a *.ses file.

The statement has two forms:

1. Form 1:

```
From the <perspective> perspective, <component or coupled model>
sends <Message> to all <component>!
```

where <component> should already have been specified as a component derived by restructuting of a multiaspect in the <perspective>> (see the "Restructure SES" entry.)

<Message> can be any alphabetic string - a matching pair of ouput and input ports are auto-generated if it does not already exist.

```
From   the   game   perspective,   Simon   sends   DoCommand   to   all
Player!
```
which says that Simon's output port outDoCommand is coupled to every Player's input port inDoCommand.

```
From the game perspective, Game sends StartUp to all Player!
```

which says that Game's input port inStartUp is coupled to every Player's input port inStartUp.

2. Form 2:

```
From   the   <perspective>   perspective,   <component   or   coupled
model> sends <outPort1> to all <component1> as <inPort2>!
```

where <component1> should already have been specified as a component derived by restructuting of a multiaspect in the <perspective>.

Here <inPort1> and <inPort2> are input ports of <coupled model> and <component> respectively.

Other Comments:

• The semantics of "sends to all" and "sends to each" are similar but not identical.
• The difference between these statements is that "sends to each" creates a port for each receiver at the sender and couples these in one–one fashion.

- This allows sending a different, customized, message to each receiver.
- For example, Simon sends the same command to all the players, but only sends youAreOut to those who have failed to comply.
- Note that Form 1 is a short hand way of writing Form 2 where the <Message> string gives rise to the pair of ports with the same name, <inMessage> for <coupled model> and its <component>.
- Form 2 allows you to explicitly state the ports involved in a coupling.
- You must use it when the ports you are coupling do not share a common suffix, <Message> nor do they have prefixes "in".

2.9 Topic: The "Sends" (Internal Coupling) Statement in SES

Why use it:

A series of these statements tells how the components of a coupled model are coupled. i.e., how their output and input ports are connected together.

When to use it:

Write this kind of statement when you want to specify how a component's output port is coupled to some other component's input port.

How to use it:

The statement has two forms:

1. Form 1:

```
From the <perspective> perspective, <component1> sends <Message>
to <component2>!
```

where <component1> and <component2> should already have been specified as components in the <perspective>.

```
<Message> can be any alphabetic string - a matching pair of
ouput and input ports are auto-generated if it does not already
exist.
```

as in SimonSaySeS.txt:

```
From the play perspective, Simon sends DoCommand to Alice!
```

which says that Simon's output port outDoCommand is coupled to Alice's input port inDoCommand.

2. Form 2:

```
From the <perspective> perspective, <component1> sends <outPort>
to <component2> as <inPort>!
```

where <component1> and <component2> should already have been specified as components in the <perspective>. Here <outPort> and <inPort> are output and input ports of <component1> and <component2> respectively.

As in SimonSaySeS.txt:

```
From the play perspective, Simon sends DoCommand to Alice!
```

which says that Simon's output port outDoCommand is coupled to Alice's input port inDoCommand.

Other Comments:

- Note that Form 1 is a short hand way of writing Form 2 where the <Message> string gives rise to the pair of ports, <outMessage> and <inMessage>.
- Form 2 allows you to explicitly state the ports involved in a coupling. You must use it when the ports you are coupling do not share a common suffix, <Message>, nor do they have prefixes "in" and "out".

2.10 Topic: The "Sends" (External Input Coupling) statement in SES

Why use it:

A series of these statements tells how the input ports of a coupled model are coupled to input ports of its components

When to use it:

Write this kind of statement when you want to specify how an input port of the coupled model is coupled to the input port of some component.

How to use it:

The statement has two forms:

1. Form 1:

```
From the <perspective> perspective, <coupled model> sends
<Message> to <component>!
```

where <component> should already have been specified as a component in the <perspective>.

<Message> can be any alphabetic string—a matching pair of ouput and input ports are auto-generated if it does not already exist.

as in LatencyMeasurementSeS.txt:

```
From the overall perspective, LatencyMeasurement sends StartUp
to Starter!
```

which says that LatencyMeasurement's input port inStartUp is coupled to Starter's input port inStartUp.

2. Form 2:

```
From the <perspective> perspective, <coupled model> sends
<inPort1> to <component> as <inPort2>!
```

where <component> should already have been specified as a component in the <perspective>. Here <inPort1> and <inPort2> are input ports of <coupled model> and <component> respectively.

as in SimonSaySeS.txt:

From the play perspective, Simon sends DoCommand to Alice !

which says that Simon's output port outDoCommand is coupled to Alice's input port inDoCommand.

Other Comments:

- Note that Form 1 is a short hand way of writing Form 2 where the <Message> string gives rise to the pair of ports with the same name, <inMessage> for <coupled model> and its <component>.
- Form 2 allows you to explicitly state the ports involved in a coupling. You must use it when the ports you are coupling do not share a common suffix, <Message> nor do they have prefixes "in".

2.11 Topic: The "Sends" (External Output Coupling) Statement in SES

Why use it:

A series of these statements tell how the output ports of a coupled model are coupled to output ports of its components.

When to use it:

Write this kind of statement when you want to specify how an output port of a component is coupled to the output port of the coupled model in which it resides.

How to use it:

Write the statement into a *.ses file:

The statement has two forms:

1. Form 1:

```
From  the <perspective> perspective, <component> sends <Message>
to <coupled model>!
```

where <component> should already have been specified as a component in the <perspective>.

<Message> can be any alphabetic string—a matching pair of output ports are auto-generated if they do not already exist.

For example,

```
From the overall perspective, Reporter sends Report to Network!
```

which says that Reporter 's output port outReport is coupled to Network's output port outReport (where Reporter is a component of Network.)

2. Form 2:

```
From the <perspective> perspective, <component> sends <outPort1>
to <coupled model> as <outPort2>!
```

where <component> should already have been specified as a component in the <perspective>.

Here <outPort1> and <outPort2> are output ports of <component> and <coupled model> respectively.

For example,

```
From the overall perspective, Reporter sends outReport to Network
as outReport!
```

which says that Reporter 's output port outReport is coupled to Network's output port outReport (where Reporter is a component of Network.)

Other Comments:

- Note that Form 1 is a short hand way of writing Form 2 where the <Message> string gives rise to the pair of ports with the same name, <outMessage>, for the <coupled model> and its <component>.
- Form 2 allows you to explicitly state the ports involved in a coupling.
- You must use Form 2 when the ports you are coupling are not of the form out <Message>.

2.12 Topic: The "Sends" (Internal Coupling) Statement in SES

Why use it:

A series of these statements tells how the components of a coupled model are coupled. i.e., how their output and input ports are connected together.

When to use it:

Write this kind of statement when you want to specify how a component's output port is coupled to some other component's input port.

How to use it:

The statement has two forms:

1. Form 1:

```
From the <perspective> perspective, <component1> sends <Message>
to <component2>!
```

where <component1> and <component2> should already have been specified as components in the <perspective>.

`<Message>` can be any alphabetic string -a matching pair of ouput and input ports are auto-generated if it does not already exist.

as in SimonSaySeS.txt:

From the play perspective, Simon sends DoCommand to Alice!

which says that Simon's output port outDoCommand is coupled to Alice's input port inDoCommand.

2. Form 2:

From the `<perspective>` perspective, `<component1>` sends `<outPort>` to `<component2>` as `<inPort>`!

where `<component1>` and `<component2>` should already have been specified as components in the `<perspective>`. Here `<outPort>` and `<inPort>` are output and input ports of `<component1>` and `<component2>` respectively.

As in SimonSaySeS.txt:

From the play perspective, Simon sends DoCommand to Alice!

which says that Simon's output port outDoCommand is coupled to Alice's input port inDoCommand.

Other Comments:

- Note that Form 1 is a short hand way of writing Form 2 where the `<Message>` string gives rise to the pair of ports, `<outMessage>` and `<inMessage>`.
- Form 2 allows you to explicitly state the ports involved in a coupling. You must use it when the ports you are coupling do not share a common suffix, `<Message>`, nor do they have prefixes "in" and "out".

2.13 Topic: The System Entity Structure (Introduction)

Why use it:
The System Entity Structure (SES) provides easier user-friendly means to define coupled models than writing directly in code. An SES without specializations is automatically transformed into coded form to create a coupled model.

When to use it:
Define an SES when you need to create a coupled model that can run on its own.
Subsequently, the SES can be extended to elaborate this coupled model into a family of coupled models.

How to use it:
Write various natural language statements.in a *.ses file/

Other Comments:

- Individual statements are discussed on separate entries.
- Compare the individual statements with the corresponding features in the *java files to gain a thorough understanding of how they fit together.

2.14 Topic: Variables in SES

Why use variables:

- Variables can be attached to entities in an SES. An attached variable can be assigned a specification of the values it can assume called its range specification.
- Such a variable can also be assigned an initial value from this set, called its default value.
- Attached variables are inherited in the same way that aspects and specializations are.
- When a pruned entity structure is transformed into a DEVS model, the variables attached to an entity become instance variables of the model class; the default values become initial values of the associated instance variable.

The construct of a "common" variable, allows attaching a variable of the same name and range specification to each of the entities in an SES. These variables take on real numbers so that they are aggregated by addition in bottom-up fashion.

When to use variables:

- Use attached variables to define instance variables that can be manipulated in the corresponding DEVS models.
- Different default values can also be set for specialization selections so that they characterize the corresponding DEVS models.
- Common variables, such as weight and cost, are automatically aggregated so that different summed values represent the different weights, costs, etc. of different pruned structures or architectures.

How to use variables:

In the SES file write statements:

```
<entity> has <variable1>,..., <variableN-1> and <variableN>!
```

For example,

```
vehicle has horsepower, VIN, and id!
the range of <entity>'s <variable> is <type>!
```
For example,
```
the range of vehicle's horsepower is double!
the range of vehicle's id is String!
set <entity>'s <variable> to <value>!
```

For example,

```
set vehicle's horsepower to 240!
add common variable <variable>!
```

For example,
```
add common variable weight!
```

Other Comments:

- Default values for each entity's variables can be set using the "set..." statement, whether or not attached using the "add common" statement.
- "Set tall_person's height to 70!" is processed as "set tall's height to 70!" This allows pruned choices to have different values, e.g., short_person could have height set to 50.

Chapter 3
Pruning SES List

Abstract This chapter lists statements for selecting aspects and entities from specializations in System Entity Structures. The resulting pruned structures can be transformed into executable hierarchical coupled models. Also it provides statements for restructuring multi-aspects and specifying uniform couplings for such restructured aspects.

3.1 Topic: Coupling Specification for Multi-aspect Models

Why use it:

Just as restructuring a multi-aspect using a specialization with multiplicity setting allows you to determine the number components when pruning, so Coupling Specification allows you to specify couplings for the components also at the time of pruning.

When to use it:

Apply this construct to specify a coupling recipe declaratively rather than manually.

How to use it:

1. Step 1:

In a *.ses file add one or more coupling specifications as components to a coupled model containing a multi-aspect

```
From the <perspective> perspective, <coupled model> is made of
<components>, <identifier1> CouplingSpecification, …, and <identifierN>
CouplingSpecification!
```

where <components> has a multi-aspect decomposition using a specialization that will be expanded.

For example:

```
From the cell perspective, cellspace is made of cells, cellEW-
CouplingSpecification, and cellNSCouplingSpecification!
From the multiCell perspective, cells is made of more than one
cell!
cell can be x or y in location!
```

2. Step 2:

In a *.pes file, after "restructuring" and "set multiplicity" statements, write statements of the form:

```
write coupling specification for <component> and <specialization>
based on <identifier>!
for <identifier> left <identifier> sends <message> to right
<identifier>!
...
write <specification type> specification for <component> and
<specialization> based on <identifier>!
```

where <component> is the multi- entity of <components>, <specialization> is the specialization to be expanded, <identifier> is the identifier used to identify this coupling specification in the SES, <message> is a port of your choice (there may be any number of these messages), and <specification type> is a designation for an available type of coupling specification, such as "cellular" or "tree".

For example:

after the statements:

```
restructure multi-aspects using location!
set multiplicity of location as [3,3] for cell!
```

we have:

```
write coupling specification for cell and location based on
cellEW!
for cellEW leftcellEW sends East to rightcellEW!
for cellEW rightcellEW sends West to leftcellEW!
write cellular specification for cell and location based on
cellEW!
```

This sets up a coupling pattern in which cells communicate with their immediate neighbors to the east and west using ports labeled outEast, inEast, outWest, and inWest.

There is also a specification identified by cellNS, that sets up a similar north–south pattern.

Other Comments:

3.2 Topic: The "If Select" Conditional Pruning Statement

Why use it:

Use this statement to force the selection of an alternative from a specialization based on one already determined.

The second selection is conditional on the other selection and is automatically enforced when the latter is put into effect.

When to use it:

Use this statement when you want to automatically select an alternative from a specialization based on another selection.

How to use it:

The conditional statement has similar forms to the unconditional one except that uses an if.. then construction, e.g.,

```
if select <alternative> from <specialization> for <entity>
then    select    <alternative1>    from    <specialization1>    for
<entity1>!
```

where <alternative> is one of the entities under the <specialization> for the <entity> and

<alternative1> is one of the entities under the <specialization1> for the <entity1>

The conditional statement is associated with the SES itself and is placed in a *.ses file,

Example:

```
if select fast from frequency for GeneratorOfJobs then select
long from processing for ProcessorOJobs!
```

and

```
if select slow from frequency for GeneratorOfJobs then select
short from processing for ProcessorOJobs!
```

This pair of statements covers the unconditional selections of fast or slow for frequency of the generator.

If fast is selected then automatically long will be selected for processing for the processor, similarly for slow.

The effect is to constrain the selection of combinations of alternatives for the pair of specializations.

Other Comments:

Conditional pruning can be used to constrain combinations or configurations of architectures that are desired or feasible that would otherwise have to be done manually.

3.3 Topic: The Inherit Pruning Statement

Why use it:

The transformation process, not only supports re-use of models in a model repository, it also allows you to employ inheritance mechanisms to modify the behavior of the resulting component under control of the pruning process. Use the "inherit" statement to specify which classes will be employed as base classes for inheritance in the transformation process. These classes must be present in the folder *.Models.java which serves as the model repository.

See the explanation of inheritance below.

When to use it:

Include this statement type in a *.pes file that contains pruning directives.

How to use it:

The "inherit" statement takes the following forms:

`inherit from <component>` -- directs the transformation process to employ this component as a base class for inheritance.This also has a side effect that the component class will not be overwritten in postprocessing when class files are generated.

`inherit from all`-- is equivalent to specifying inheritance for each of the specialization parents in the SES.

Example:

`inherit from genr!`

To understand the inheritance process, assume that the SES file, *.ses, includes a specialization for genr which can be fast or slow in frequency!

Accordingly a pruning selection specification might be:

`select fast from frequency for genr!`

- This causes the AtomicModel class fast_gener to be created in the transformation process.
- Now, the "inherit from genr" statement above will cause fast_genr to be a derived class of genr, i.e., its class file will have the phrase "extends genr."
- This will initially cause fast_genr to behave like genr becuase all of its defining DEVS methods will be inherited from genr.
- However, it also sets up a situation in which you can override some of genr's features in the fast_gener class file to make it behave more particularly like a fast generator as opposed to say a slow generator which would be the alternative you might employ for the result slow_genr.
- Another way to cause differential behaviors in the specialized classes is based on the fact that the name of the specialized class is transmitted via its zero argument constructor to the base class via its single argument constructor.
- You can use this name, e.g., "fast_prune" to configure the base class appropriately.
- See genr.java for an example where the incoming specialization name is employed to set the interarrival time parameter corresponding to fast or slow frequency.

Similar considerations hold for the alternative to inhertance from genr, namely, inheritance from fast, a child, rather than, a parent of the specialization.

In this case, of course, fast must be a class in the repository.

Another alternative is that inheritance is not specified for a component. In this case, a Atomic or class will be generated on the spot without any more specialized behaviors.

Other Comments:

In the case of multiple specializations under the same parent, the resulting name will reflect the multiple selections. The transformation process will select the first specialization entity to have been designated in an inheritance statement. When not specified, the default inheritance source is the parent, e.g., fast_genr will inherit from genr.

3.4 Topic: Restructure SES Statement

Why use it:

The multi-aspects in a SES have to be expanded in order to prune them. This statement uses restructuring to perform this expansion.

When to use it:

Apply this statement as the first in a *.pes file to restructure the SES.

How to use it:

```
restructure multiaspects using <specialization>!
```

Each of the designated specialization entities is employed to name a copy of the multiaspect entity which is attached to the parent aspect.

Example:

```
restructure multiaspects using topic!
```

where in the *.ses file

```
From the shelf perspective, library is made of books and
librarian!
From the multiBook perspective, books is made of more than one
book!

book can be fiction or science in topic!
```

removes books from the shelf aspect of library and replaces it with the entities fiction_book and science_book. Any substructure of book is added to fiction_book and science_book.

Other Comments:

To specify restructuring of more than one multi-aspect, use the form:

```
restructure multiaspects using <specialization> then <special-
ization1> then <specialization2>…!
```

To enable a variable number of entities in a specialization for use in multi-aspect restructuring see the "Set Multiplicity" statement.

3.5 Topic: The "Select Aspect" Pruning Statement

Why use it:

Use this statement to introduce an element of choice into the sets of components that form a coupled model.

In contrast to the "Select Entity" pruning operation, this statement allows you to select from alternative aspects, i.e., sets of components and their coupling.

When to use it:

Use this kind of statement when you want to pick an alternative aspect (set of components and their couplings) for a coupled model.

Of course, the choices would have had to set up by the addition of aspects (see the "MadeOf" statement.)

How to use it:

Add this statement to a *.pes file.

The statement has two forms:

1. Form 1:

```
select <perspecive> from aspects for <entity>!
```

For example,

```
select physical from aspects for book!
```

where the physical aspect has been added to book in a *.ses file:

```
From the physical perspective, book is made of covers and pages!
```

2. Form 2:

```
select <perspecive> from aspects for <entity> under <parent>!
```

For example,

```
select bilateral from aspects for body under husband!
```

Note that the context, in this case "under husband" plays the same role it did in the "Select Entity" statement.

Other Comments:

See comments in the "Select Entity" entry.

3.6 Topic: The "Select Entity" Pruning Statement

Why use it:

Use this statement to choose one of the alternatives for a component that can be made in pruning.

Of course, the choices would have had to set up by the definition of a special-ization (see the "CanBe" statement.)

When to use it:

Use this statement when you want to select an alternative from a specialization.

How to use it:

Add this statement to a *.pes file.

The statement has two forms:

1. Form 1:

```
select <alternative> from <specialization> for <parent entity>!
```

where <alternative> is one of the entities under the <specialization> for the <parent entity>

For example,

```
select Fast from speed for GeneratorOfJobs!
```

selects Fast from the speed specialization under GeneratorOfJobs!

2. Form 2:

```
select <alternative> from <specialization> for <parent entity> under <grandparent>!
```

For example:

```
select fat from weight for body under husband!
```

which says that fat is selected from weight for the body under the parent husband.

Such contextual information is required whenever there are multiple occurrences of a specialization and you want to make different choices for different occurrences.

For example,

```
select thin from weight for body under wife!
```

The context parent can be extended to a path upwards from the entity to an ancestor such that the path uniquely distinguishes the occurrence.

For example, in

```
select large from size for muscle under rightArm under body
under husband!
```

```
select normal from size for muscle under rightArm under body
under wife!
```

distinguishes the husband's muscle from that of the wife.

Other Comments:

- The sequence of successive ancestor entities specifies the context to which the selection applies.

- In the example, the sequence rightArm,body,husband places the muscle in question as owned by husband as opposed to a similar sequence ending in wife.
- In general, the longer the sequence, the more specific the context is and the fewer possible occurrences match that context.
- In processing the pruning directives, the contexts (sequences) are ordered by decreasing length, so that more specific ones are processed first.

3.7 Topic: The "Set Multiplicity" Statement

Why use it:

While a specialization offers a selection of entities as choices, this set is fixed. However, often we would like to have this set to be adjustable to particular circumstances. For example, the restructure statement expands a multi-aspect in an SES based on the selection set in a specialization under the multi-entity.

Unfortunately, to change the number of replications of the multi-entity would require you to redefine the specialization to change the selection set. Instead of changing the SES, as this approach requires, we would rather keep the SES fixed and be able to prune it to determine the number of replications.

The "Set Multiplicity" statement enables us to do this by letting us change the number of entities in a specialization's selection set.

When to use it:

Write this statement in a pruned entity file. When the specialization in question is to support restructuring a multi-aspect, write it after the multi-aspect restructure statement

How to use it:

Write in a *.pes file:

```
set multiplicity of <specialization> as <multiplicity> for <parent
entity>!
```

where <parent entity> is the parent entity of the specialization, and <multiplicity> is one of [K] or [K,L] or [K,L,M] where K,L, and M are positive integers. The choice of dimension (1,2, or 3) should correspond to number of entities in the specialization selection set.

Also, here <specialization> is restricted to one in which its selection set are children that are leaf entities.

This causes replacement of the specialization's children by a set of entities each labeled by a string representing a point in the vector space spanned by the original children's names and the given dimensions.

For example, if the *.pes file contains:

```
set multiplicity of index as [3] for Person!
```

and the *.ses file contains:

```
Person can be id in index!
```

then after processing, the index will have children id0_Person, id1_Person, and id2_Person.

Using this statement to support restructuring of a multi-aspect is illustrated by:

```
set multiplicity of location as [3,2] for cell!
```

Here location has entities named x and y, so its six new children are cell_x0y0,cell_x1y0,...,cell_x2y1. These become the names of the cells replacing the multi-aspect for cells.

Other Comments:

- To change the number of replications of the cell, you change the dimension part of the "Set Multiplicity" statement. Note that this is a pruning, rather than an SES, operation.
- For more on restructuring go to the "Restructure SES Statement."

3.8 Topic: The "Set Name of Model" Pruning Statement

Why use it:

Use the "set" statement to rename the Java model that is generated from pruning and transforming.

When to use it:

The name of the model to be generated is automatically requested from you in the pruning interface.

How to use it:

Write the following into a *.pes file (or let the pruner request it)

```
set name of model as <name>!
```

Example:

```
set entity to prune as Truck!
```

Other Comments:

The name requested by the pruner actually appends it to the SES root name.

Chapter 4
Miscellaneous List

Abstract This chapter lists approaches to testing atomic and coupled models as well as creating java classes for use in models.

4.1 Topic: Testing Atomic Models

Why use it:

An atomic model can have complicated logic and state transition structure which leads to complex behavior.

It is typically not possible to verify that the model carries out the behavior you expect by inspection, so a more disciplined approach is advisable.

The Atomic Model interface includes methods that make it easier to test atomic models.

Models generated from FDDEVS automatically include invocation of these methods; they can also be written manually using the same patterns as in these files.

When to use it:

After creating an atomic model (from an FDDEVS - see "FDDEVS Models" or manually), you need to test to verify that it carries out the behavior you expect.

How to use it:

This process has two forms:

1. Form 1

The source code for your atomic model in Java includes a main routine of the following form:

```
MyAtomicModel model = new MyAtomicModel();
Simulation sim = new
com.ms4systems.devs.core.simulation.impl.SimulationImpl(
" MyAtomicModel Simulation", model);
sim.startSimulation(0);
sim.simulateIterations(Long.MAX_VALUE);
}
```

B. P. Zeigler, *Guide to Modeling and Simulation of Systems of Systems*,   39
SpringerBriefs in Computer Science, DOI: 10.1007/978-1-4471-4570-7_4,
© Bernard P. Zeigler 2013

where MyAtomicModel is the atomic model class you are testing.

Notes:

- only the class of the model need change in the above form.
- use the form as it stands to test the model in its initial state with no input.
- repeat the segment after the initialize() statement to test from the state reached by the executing the first segment.
- the form is automatically generated by the FDDEVS generation process.

2. Form 2:

Using the simulation viewer (SimViewer), display the model and employ the available buttons to test the model.

Test buttons and associated operations include:

- **Step button**—moves the model from the current state to its next state due to the internal transition function. You see message exchanges for the transition.
- **Run button**—executes successive internal transitions until the model reaches a passive state or paused by the step button
- **Run until button**—executes successive internal transitions until the model reaches a passive state or stopped by the elapsed time or number of transitions specified
- **View button**—executes successive internal transitions until the model reaches a passive state or paused by the step button shows the message exchanges in each step
- **Restart button**—returns the model to its initial state

Other Comments:

- To inject a message into an input port, right click on the model box and make a selection from the pop up menu.

4.2 Topic: Testing Coupled Models

Why use it:

A coupled model is the result of coupling together component models, each of which may have its own complex behavior. So the result may exhibit even more complex behavior and is typically not possible to verify that the coupled model carries out the behavior you expect by inspection, so a more disciplined approach is advisable.

When to use it:

After creating a coupled model (from an SES or manually), you need to test to verify that it carries out the behavior you expect.

How to use it:

This process has two forms:

1. Form 1

The source code for your atomic model in Java includes a main routine of the following form:

```
MyCoupledModel model = new MyCoupledModel ();
Simulation sim = new
com.ms4systems.devs.core.simulation.impl.SimulationImpl("My-
CoupledModel Simulation",model);
sim.startSimulation(0);
sim.simulateIterations(Long.MAX_VALUE);
}
```

where MyCoupledModel is the coupled model class you are testing.

Notes:

- only the class of the model need change in the above form.
- use the form as it stands to test the model in its initial state with no input.
- repeat the segment after the initialize() statement to test from the state reached by the executing the first segment.
- the form is automatically generated by the FDDEVS generation process.

2. Form 2:

Using the simulation viewer, display the model and employ the available buttons to test the model.

Test buttons and associated operations include:

- **Step button**—moves the model from the current state to its next state due to the internal transition function. You see message exchanges for the transition.
- **Run button**—executes successive internal transitions until the model reaches a passive state or paused by the step button
- **Run until button**—executes successive internal transitions until the model reaches a passive state or stopped by the elapsed time or number of transitions specified
- **View button**—executes successive internal transitions until the model reaches a passive state or paused by the step button—. shows the message exchanges in each step
- **Restart button**—returns the model to its initial state

Other Comments:

- to inject a message into an input port, right click on the model box and make a selection from the pop up menu.

4.3 Topic: Java Class Definition

Why use it:

Create a Java class if you need to send a message that needs a more complex data structure than a string or when you need to keep track of structured data as an instance variable in the state of a model.

When to use it:

Create a Java class after you have developed an atomic model and wish to have it send or receive structured data messages or work with complex data in its state.

How to use it:

In a *.dnl file write

```
A <JavaClass> has a <var1> ,a <var2> ,…,and a <var3>!
```

where `<JavaClass>` is the class you wish to define and where each name in the list is to be an instance variable of the class. To give the type of an instance variable and (optionally) a default value, write

```
The   range   of   <JavaClass>'s   <var>   is   <type>   with   default
"<defaultValue>"!
```

A file JavaClass.java will be automatically generated with the given instance variable declarations. Also constructors for the class and setter and getter methods will be defined for each of the instance variables. For example,

```
A WorkToDo has id, processingTime, and startTime!
the range of WorkToDo's id is int and default "0"!
the range of WorkToDo's processingTime is double!
the range of WorkToDo's startTime is double!
```

Other Comments

To see how to use a Java class object in messages go to the entry "Sending/ Receiving DEVS messages."

To see how to use a Java class object in an atomic model go to the entry "Declaring instance variables."

Index